TO BE BORN

BOOK OF
POEMS

BY
TISHA

FIRST EDITION

CREATED AND EDITED BY TISHA
4403 N. SACRAMENTO AVENUE
CHICAGO, IL 60625

PRINTED BY CREATESPACE

(FIRST EDITION)

ISBN-13: 978-0615899084 (TISHA)
ISBN-10: 0615899080

DEDICATIONS:

THANK YOU TO
HESAKETVMESE/GOD
WHO GIVES US ALL BREATH.

THANK YOU TO
MY MUSCOGEE CREEK ANCESTORS
WHO DWELL AMONGST
THE TREES AND THE WIND.

THANK YOU STORMY CLOUD
FOR YOUR INSPIRATION AND SUPPORT.

CONTENTS:

ACKNOWLEDGEMENTS:

THANK YOU ALL FOR SHARING

YOUR TIME WITH ME,

ALLOWING MY HUMBLE SPIRIT

ANOTHER CHANCE TO "HECKETV"

TO BE BORN

WITH GRATITUDE, "MVTO/THANK YOU".

LITTLE ROBIN

LITTLE ROBIN DON'T YOU
CRY.
I AM WALKING BY AND
BY.
I HEAR YOU,
YOUR SORROW BINDS,
INTO MY HEART,
INTO MY
MIND.
YOUR RED BROW,
TOUCHES MY RED
HEART
AND
FOREVER WE SHALL
AND
NEVER PART.
LITTLE ROBIN
FORGET
ME NOT TODAY,
THIS PLACE,
THIS MOMENT,
THIS SPOT.

THE STREET DRAGON

LEE STREET DRAGONFLY

ONE OF YOU HAS CHECKERBOARD
WINGS, LIKE AN
AIRPLANE IN FLIGHT.
YOU SWOOP BY,
I START TO CRY.
WHY WOULD ANYONE
WANT TO HURT YOU?
TAKE CARE MY FRIEND
AND KEEP FLYING HIGH AND FREE,
YOU ARE MY HERO.

AUTUMN TREE

AUTUMS COOL IS UPON US
AS WE AWAIT THE BITTER COLD OF
WINTER.
THE LEAVES STILL EMPLOY OUR SENSES
AND WE ARE LUCKY TO BE AMONGST THEM
ONCE AGAIN. I HOPE TO GREET YOU
TODAY AND SHARE MY BREATH WITH
YOURS.
I KNOW YOU AND YOU KNOW ME,
MY DEAR FRIEND,
ARE YOU FROM MY HOME? I THINK MAYBE.
I THINK OF YOU AND I AM
PEACEFUL.
I WILL SEE YOU AGAIN AND MAYBE YOUR LEAVES
WILL BE GONE TO THE LAND IN
WHICH THEY CAME. BUT, I WILL REMEMBER YOUR
BEAUTY, AT
WHICH I TRIED TO CAPTURE IN A PAINTING.
I WISH I COULD STILL SEE YOUR ELEGANCE.
TODAY, TOMORROW. WILL I HAVE TIME?
STAND STILL IN TIME MY FRIEND, I WILL BE THERE.

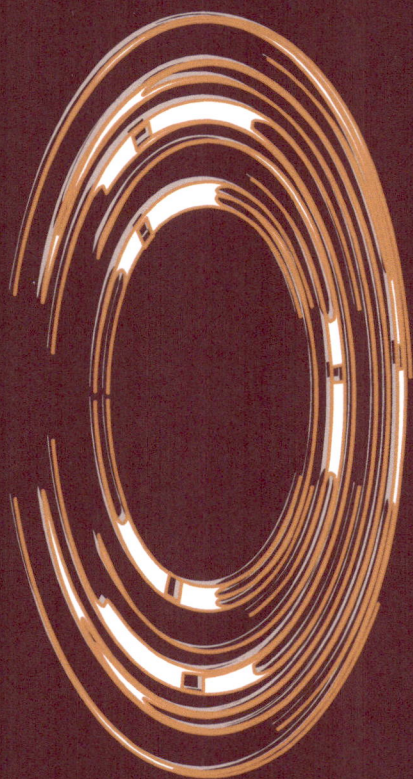

YOUTH

WHEN I WAS YOUNG........
(FILL IN THE BLANKS WITH YOUR MIND,

A SIMPLE
THOUGHT / FEELING
PROVOKING IDEA.

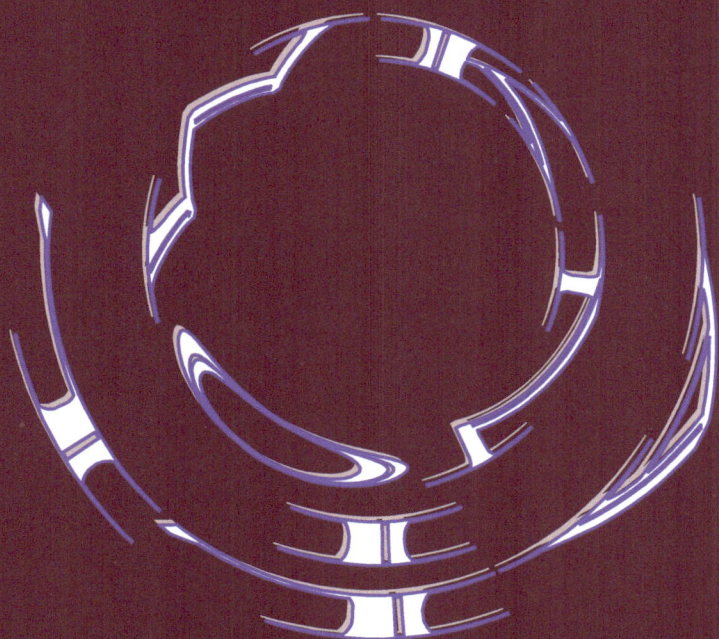

ALL I KNOW

THE WILLOWS BLOW
AND SO THEY SHOW,
MY HEART CONNECTED
TO MY EYE.

FOR ALL I KNOW
IS WHAT I KNOW,
A BRIEF ENCOUNTER
WITH MY SKY.

FOR WHAT I SEE
I DO NOT KNOW,
WHAT AILS MY HEART
SO DEEP.

FOR ALL I KNOW

IS WHAT I KNOW,

AND WHAT I KNOW

DOES FLEET.

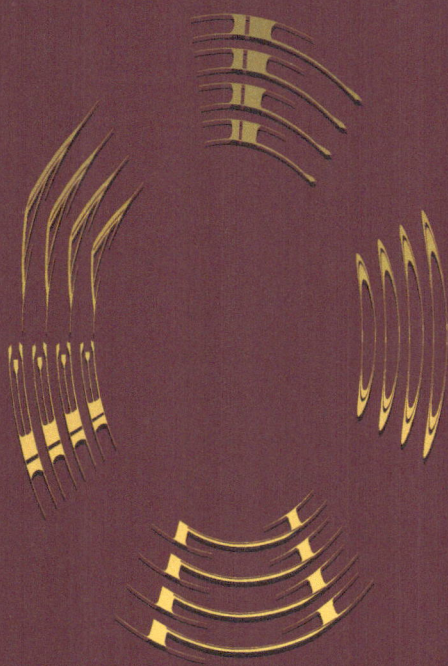

ALONE

MY WORLD, MY EYES, MY BREATH,
MY COURAGE,
IS SKEWED BY PAIN.

ALL OTHERS MUST SEE THE WORLD
THROUGH THEIR OWN EYES.
NO MORE CAN I INTERCEDE.

I AM ALONE NOW,

YOU ARE TO.

SKIN OF THE TREE

AS WINTER

IS TO

TREES, WINTER

IS TO

SKIN. DRY,

BARREN, BRITTLE,

BUDS APPEAR,

BUT DO

NOT BLOSSOM.

APPARENT BEAUTY

UNDERNEATH, WITHIN.

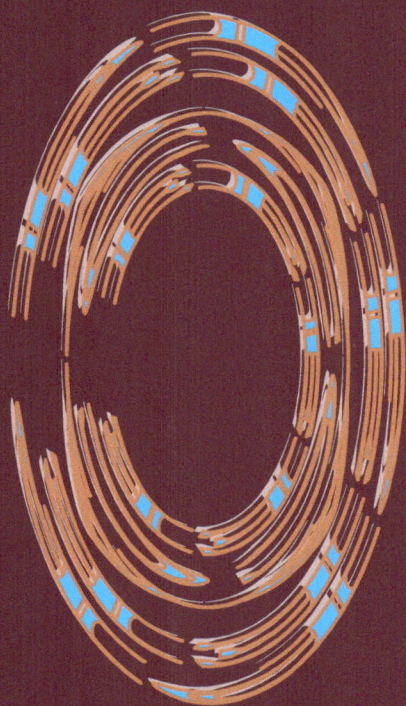

PEACE

I LOOK
FOR PEACE
IN THE STREETS,
I LOOK FOR PEACE IN MY LIFE,
I LOOK FOR PEACE UNDERNEATH,
BUT ALL AROUND THERE IS STRIFE.
UP HIGH, DOWN LOW AND ALL AROUND.
IN THE GREAT BOOK I LOOK FOR PEACE.
IN THE NOOKS I LOOK FOR PEACE.
WHERE ARE YOU? MY FRIEND.
SOMEBODY KNOWS, ABOUT PEACE, HAVE
YOU
FORGOTTEN US? HERE IS WHERE I LIVE,
HERE IS WHERE I BREATHE,
I'M RIGHT HERE, HEY OVER HERE, PLEASE,
S.O.S,
(SCREAM) I'M HERE POUNDING MY CHEST,
FOR US
ALL.
SORRY NOT YOUR TIME LITTLE GIRL,
SORRY NOT YOUR TIME, YOUNG LADY,
SORRY NOT YOUR TIME MIDDLE AGED
WOMEN.
SORRY NOT YOUR TIME, HUES OF MAN.
IT'S NOT YOUR TIME (SCREAM).
BUT WHEN? WHEN WILL IT BE OUR TIME,
TOMORROW, NEXT WEEK, HOW ABOUT
TODAY! (SCREAM) TODAY!

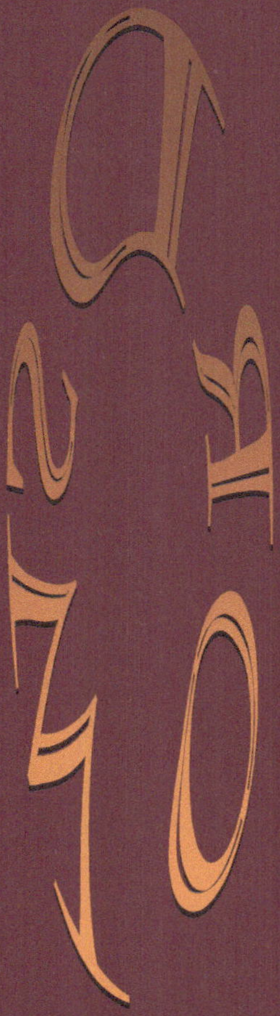

WORDS

AS WORDS CROSS
THE PAGES, SO
DO MY DREAMS
OF A BETTER
DAY, A BETTER
TOMORROW, WITH LESS
SADNESS AND TEARS.
A WISH FOR
MORE LAUGHTER AND
SUN. A PLESANTNESS
OF LIFE THAT
ONLY A FEW
CAN TRULY SAY
THEY HAVE LIVED.
I WANT THIS
FOR MYSELF, FOR
OTHERS, FOR ALL
LIVING SPECIES. FOR
IN US ALL
IS THIS PRIMAL
PEACE,
A SOFTENING OF
THE BLOWS OF
LIFE. WITHIN, UNDERNEATH,
ONTO, OUTSIDE, FOREVER
AND ALWAYS TOOTH
AND NAIL, WE
ARE HERE, WE
ARE
ONE.

TO HUG A BIRDS BOSOM

OH HOW I WOULD
LOVE TO HUG A
BIRDS BOSOM,
SO SOFT, SO GENTLE, SO SAFE.
FROM THE BEATING OF
IT'S LITTLE HEART,
COMES THE BEATING
OF A GIANT,
TO FLY WITH AND AGAINST THE
WIND.
THE PEACEFULNESS OF YOUR EXISTENCE
OVERWHELMS ME AT TIMES.
FOR YOU LITTLE BIRD ARE SO SMALL AND
VULNERABLE
IT SEEMS. I WORRY FOR YOU AND PRAY FOR
YOU
EACH DAY THAT YOU WILL BE PROTECTED
AND
WILL
ALWAYS FIND
YOUR WAY.
FOR IN YOU IS HOPE FOR A
NEW DAY.
YOU KNOW WHEN THE
WORLD IS READY
FOR GODS SPLENDOR.
YOU KNOW WHERE
THE WIND BLOWS. YOU
KNOW THE
SORROW OF THE WORLD.
THE GENTLE EYE OF THE
BEHOLDER IS IN YOU. FOR
PEACE IS IN YOU AND
THEREFORE IN ME.

IF YOU ONLY KNEW

IF YOU ONLY KNEW THE TIME, EFFORT
AND SHEER ENERGY IT TAKES TO LET
DOWN MY WALL, MY FORT, MY STEEL
ENCASEMENT, MY ENCLOSED TOMB. THEN
YOU WOULD KNOW THAT MY TIME, EFFORT
AND SHEER ENERGY WILL HAVE BEEN AND MOST
LIKELY WILL END IN DEPLETION ONE DAY, I WILL NOT
BE ABLE TO LET THE WALL DOWN AGAIN,
BRICK BY BRICK,
STEEL BEAM, BY BEAM, CEMENT BARRIER, ONE BY ONE.
I WILL NOT HAVE THE STRENGTH TO BUILD IT, OR
DISMANTLE IT. IF YOU ONLY KNEW HOW I
HOPED IT WILL AND CAN STAY DOWN.
THAT THE HORRORS, FEELINGS OF FEAR,
DISCONTENTMENT, AGONY, DESPAIR
AND SORROW WOULD NEVER
RETURN, SO THAT IN LIFE, I
COULD SEE THE BEAUTIFUL
VALLEYS, PRISTINE, WITH
NO WALL OR BARRIER
TO HOLD
THEM IN, NO WALLS, ENRAGED
ENEMY, CONFIDANT, TO TELL
ALL, KIND HEART, TO BURNED
SOUL. FEAR ERODES MY BLISS,
FEAR ERODES MY SILENT
TRINITY, FEAR ERODES MY
LIFE, FEAR ERODES MY
DREAMS. IF YOU
ONLY KNEW.

BUT YOU DON'T !

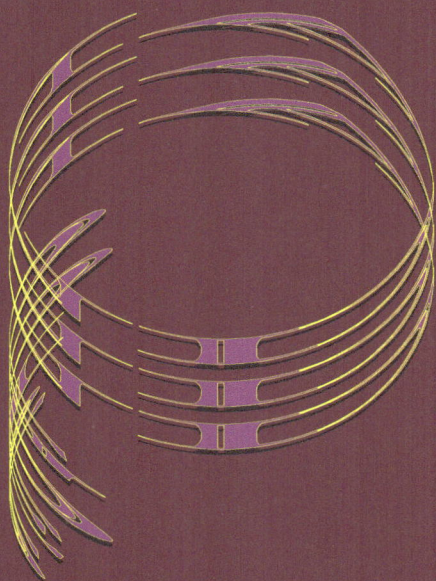

AND GOES
A PAINTER PAINTS
AND SO IT
GOES, AS COLOR
RULES, AS NIGHT
UNFOLDS.
A POET WRITES
AND SPEAKS, AND
GOES AND GOES
AND WRITES AND
GOES. A PHOTO
SNAPS, SOME HERE,
SOME THERE. A
PHOTO GRABS THE
GRAPHERS EYE, IS
NONE THE WORSE
FOR WEAR, TO
SEE IS TO
KNOW, AND GOES
AND GOES. A
SINGERS OCTAVE SHATTERING
A GLASS, AN
ARTIST SORROW, A
NATIONS GASP, AND
GOES AND GOES.
A MUSICIAN ENTERS
THEIR HARBORS HARMONY,
LOOKING FOR THE
SOUL IN THE
SWEET MELODIES
AND GOES,
AND GOES.
ALL TRYING TO CONNECT TO
THE FORCE WITHIN,
THROUGH WINTERS SHUDDER AND SPRINGS
CHIRP AND SUMMERS EN PLEIN AIR
AND THE LEAVES DO FALL
AND GOES, AND GOES.

FATHER

FOR
EACH
HIS
OWN
DOES
PONDER,
THE
SHADOW
OF
OUR
FATHERS.
THEIR
CHILLING
PRESENCE
BESTOWS.
AN
OCCURRENCE
DEEP
WITHIN
OUR
TROUBLED
HEARTS
WE
KNOW

WE

CAN FIND THEM THERE.

LOVE ONE ANOTHER

www.ingramcontent.com/pod-product-compliance
Lightning Source LLC
Chambersburg PA
CBHW041804040426
42448CB00001B/33